O, But in the Library

poems

Susan Stevens

Finishing Line Press
Georgetown, Kentucky

O, But in the Library

Copyright © 2017 by Susan Stevens
ISBN 978-1-63534-096-9 First Edition
All rights reserved under International and Pan-American Copyright Conventions.
No part of this book may be reproduced in any manner whatsoever without written permission from the publisher, except in the case of brief quotations embodied in critical articles and reviews.

ACKNOWLEDGMENTS

My thanks to the editor of the online journal *Voices on the Wind*, where these poems, or versions thereof, appeared.

The epigraph from Edith Wharton's story is translated "To understand, it is necessary to love."

Publisher: Leah Maines

Editor: Christen Kincaid

Cover photo of the Minneapolis Public Library, 2-20-2007: Steve Lyon

Author Photo: Mario Acevedo

Cover Design: Elizabeth Maines

Printed in the U SA on acid-free paper.
Order online: www.finishinglinepress.com
also available on amazon.com

Author inquiries and mail orders:
Finishing Line Press
P. O. Box 1626
Georgetown, Kentucky 40324
U. S. A.

Contents

Men in Bars 1
Its Own Magic 2
Ne Plus Ultra 3
You, Somewhere 4
Immersion 5
Mindfulness 6
Building It Up 7
Before It Gets There: The End of Postmortem Blues 8
Passing Over 9
And That's Final 10
Arguing With the Expert 11
Hazard 13
Redaction for Jim Simmerman 14
1960s Marvels 15
For the Concrete Man 16
Dead Air 17
United 18
Rhodes Scholar *(Picaro)* 19
She Finds He Is Standing Before Her 20
A Chastisement for John Donne 21
You See 23
On the Road 24
Long Shot 25
Just Divine 26
About Desire 27
Blindsided by Andrei Codrescu 28

Pour comprendre il faut aimer.

Edith Wharton, "The Muse's Tragedy"

Men in Bars

were *not* the ones
I wanted to meet
in my twenties, or ever.
O, but in the library
was my idea
of a good man.
There, I could scan
the stacks for the bright guy
in 811.08 or 811 L95Yh
(and always with glasses—
they stirred me
as half-dressed
women did men),
position myself
around the corner
from his fixed reverie,
push a book
through to his side
and onto the floor—
then run around to
retrieve it and apologize.
I waited. I had to find out
if he was as intelligent
as he was meant to be.

Its Own Magic

> *For me, you are nothing but the you that is within my world, within the universal self as my world.*
> Kōshō Uchiyama

When I call you
in my head
I use your first name
very lightly
since it is shocking to do so
even to me
(I know you
I don't know you)—
and important
that you not hear
this presumption
bumping into your ordinary
but whole, complete privacy.

Once in a hotel at 4 a. m.
you wrote *You are asleep*
and I found this intimate
that you should say it
but still your first name
only has conversance
in my head
I know you don't know you
there's a *koan* in there
I must face
without thinking about it

Ne Plus Ultra

> *Presence is more than just being there.*
> Malcolm Forbes

> *Being solitary is being alone well.*
> Alice Koller

> *Be where you are; otherwise you will miss your life.*
> the Buddha

Where I want you
is not close
is on a page
is not on a walk or a plane in a ship or even an Alfa Romeo
is in a dream or a film or the mail
but not on a hike or skates
in a court, café
or in a *tête-à-tête*.

Stay where you are—
I can always pull you off a shelf
or tune in an interview
as I praise the paradox:
hell-and-gone intimacy
shocked, finding its own level.

You, Somewhere

Feeling the distance
between us heady, keeping you
dreamily spiritual—I find
our dialogue visionary,
simply preposterous,
turning my senses
over and over in mad *eros*.

What finally happens
to the life of the mind?
Surely it is like you: somewhere.
Here I go, tripping again
in this faraway chaste discourse,
wrangling with disbelief
so palpable that I think
the you of us
is someone else.
And *somewhere*,
you with your usual ease
in learning the ropes
are again a quick study, seeing it
this way for perhaps the first time,
feeling the distance.

Immersion

Your words simmer
all around me,
a deep pool of astonishment—
then a complex network
of conceptual channels, then waves
one jump ahead of me. I cannot swim.
The spindrift resembles the way
your presence might feel.
Once revived, I want to ask (no levity now):
Are you of our ongoing script really he, the writer,
not his secretary, assistant, colleague,
friend, relative, man on the street—
someone else? You will see now just how serious
is someone's inability to manage awe.
Moving from book to book,
I see we can manage parlance
apropos of mystery and fast currents,
even without the swimming bit.

I like our distance
and will get a yacht to expand it,
to sail through the secret,
sparking evanescence.

Mindfulness

*You're like a plaintive melody
that never lets me be....*
                              Arthur Freed

Even angry, you would
see to your words with care.
You are impressive, you are erotic,
you are wildly undomesticated,
the most rational-emotive
man alive. You don't scare me.
The audience is ever more aroused
to attention: You may as well be back
in the classroom with that abiding vigor!
We see in the essays a mighty show
of candor, then for crying out loud,
it's your paradoxical shyness,
coming back like Lassie or Shane.
You make me think over my head.
And make me wonder
not how you learned the language
so fast, but how soon you came to be
this lovingly articulate.

Building It Up

> *...oxytocin is stimulated by everything from
> holding hands, to feeling supported, to orgasm.*
> Loretta Graziano Breuning

I want you to think of yourself as the man
nowhere to be found, and who rolled
the Sisyphean stone of desire uphill
for me where, curiously, it stayed put.
I want you to think of yourself
as the resuscitator of this brain's
circuit of pleasure-seekers
that hunt down willing receptors.
(Make that *eager* receptors.) I want you
to keep thinking, talking, writing,
wandering where you may,
always a friend to the proprieties and trust.
It's tantalizing when you stand
on ceremony.

Before It Gets There: The End of Postmortem Blues

> *If you don't know how to die, don't worry; Nature will tell you what to do . . . don't bother your head about it.*
> Michel de Montaigne

His deathlike experience
might inform our own
approach. Please, let's have more
of the Stoic's *amor fati*
and *ars memoriae*. —It's just like passing out,
Montaigne tells us, which we anyhow
have been known to do with our heads
in his copious *Essays*.

Take a better attitude
to death, he advises;
it only happens once—
how bad can that be?
"If you have lived a day,
you have seen everything,"
Montaigne consoles.
Would you parry his words
assuring that our regrets
for loss and wishes and this life
lose all meaning (you'll be gone)
and cease to be mourned?

Passing Over

One never comes again to the same.
                                        Osho

You, who I have decided
are my last intrigue,
have transcended the whole scene.
The dialogue, your *gemütlichkeit*,
galvanized a passel of poems
and let loose the fillip to eroticism
flourishing at a distance. Even now
your words are packing a punch somewhere
I can't hear. Yet for moments that refuse
forgetting, as Nani schooled Osho,
"never ask for more. What is, is enough."

And That's Final

Undressing before
his face
on the cover
of his book
I trust
his eyes' unblinking
appraisal
his good taste to stay put
my letting well enough
alone
and the probity of distance.
No more heroes, I say

Arguing with the Expert

Now about that novel, Syd Field tells me
in his highly acclaimed *Screenplay: The Foundations
of Screenwriting,* you must realize *character is action;
what a person* **does** *is who he is, not what he* **says**.
I want to tell him that in a novel about 1960s Alaska,
people *would* sit around talking, to the exclusion
of action. Their behavior *was* their dialogue then,
in the '60s—especially in Alaska.

But Syd knows all this; he's a veteran. (He's also
in Beverly Hills, and I need to talk to him.)
In one of his chapters, he wonders aloud
about the best way to turn other writing
into a screenplay—which, he allows, is not easy.

I want to take issue with Syd, pointing out the success
of French films like *My Night at Maud's* and *Claire's Knee*
—and America's *My Dinner with Andre,* where all the two men did
was eat and talk. And a certain niche audience ate it up.

But I have my own problems with this novel, begun at 17
some 40 years ago, since it seems that each time I pick it up,
I'm intruding in the characters' lives—perversely
curious and telling them what to say.
Obviously, they're on their own now; I see that.
Then there's the old fear of "Did I write that?
I don't remember saying that," further stressing
I'm just an interloper here.

Syd—my protagonist has a maroon MGA
and gatherings at his place where people
drink espresso, listen to jazz, and talk endlessly about Zen,
Schopenhauer, art, and Proust. They worship both
sound and silence—and major in philosophy for the fun of it.
Ergo, thinking is fun, and talking about thoughts is what they do.
Endlessly, Syd.

Hazard

If you have been
there before it's still
the first time like
accretions surrounding
a burl new layers
incipient each time
new eyes plumb
yours in genesis
of where you have
already been
can't guess or
guarantee the
outcome is new no
matter how ancient
the humanity there are
no comparisons to be
made no connections
that will help
in virgin soil all
is primitive riotous
your meeting someone
else is primeval
and you must not
presuppose for that
is barbarism or drift
all is intentional
your eyes will say
all anyone presently
needs to know

Redaction for Jim Simmerman

I'm trying to think
how this life
drove you to end yours
as poet, teacher,
wry observer who once said
in a poem, "Nothing good lasts."

Another hip replacement
was ahead, your dog died,
girlfriend left—
all counterbalanced
by the awards,
karate black belt,
admiring students,
published volumes.

Still, how could you?
What antidotes
to your head games
could anyone have presumed
to offer? In some needling way
I must know why you couldn't look
farther ahead. Just a *few days*
might have done it: the paradigm shift,
an unjaded look at things, the next book
and reading, the new dog, the new girl,
your students' esteem
and homage of colleagues—
all these that could have made you
look again. Just a few days more,
to stop the gun at your head.

1960s Marvels

Upchucking each morning
as guinea pigs
for Enovid-E
we wonder if parturition
can be any worse
than this.

We intrepid marvels
are outdoing ourselves
with this regimen,
nauseated and in sync
with the gutsy pediatrician
placing *Stop at Two* brochures
in his waiting room.

For the Concrete Man

The man with the black lunchbox
is thinking. He is all geometry
as he nears the site where he knows
he is on new ground.

This man, who eschewed
touch-typing, will stop at nothing
to use both hands as he lays concrete
in shuttering. A laborer now, he imagines
writing a book on the esthetics
of Quikrete
and the satisfaction of arduous toil,
when his hands might caress
the burl in a railroad tie
or a piece of honey onyx he found
by happenstance. He is heavy on irony,
and so is the prospect
of his contemplating aggregate, control joints,
braced 2x6 wood forms, concrete floating,
then gradually moving into passive solar
though he doesn't know it yet.

Next will be Xeriscape design,
placing gargantuan boulders,
creating abstract snakes out of concrete,
and designing a water wall.
He will be a sculptor and more.
This man will stop at nothing
to use the full range of his hands;
he has stopped at nothing
at every juncture,
at every turn of phrase.

Dead Air

For him momentum
is the succession
of cued-up sides,
the glossy spin
of black vinyl
deftly slid
from its case,
and always on time

he knows when he opens
the mic
he can't use the words
he wants—
digital countdown
won't permit Roget
his paroxysm
takes too long

stand by
for the first time
ever he can't
go on
like this,
slumped over the board
with Tchaikovsky's *First*
and a Schubert trio
cued
and no one else
actually standing by
but the duffer
calling in
wanting like hell
to get on

United

> *The misfortune of marriage is the proximity of its fruit, its superabundance.*
> — Søren Kierkegaard

> *In marriage, partners settle in to something I don't like.*
> — Marie Cox

> *Whenever you want to marry someone, go have lunch with his ex-wife.*
> — Shelley Winters

And further, Woody Allen tells us that "marriage is the death of hope." But what all this is *really* about is the absence of tension.

There just *has* to be that tautness with men and women—the kind that makes them anticipate. You know what I mean: It's the desirable tension between people that somehow loses energy, turns flaccid, after people get to know one another. Keeping it there is the art; but people are pretty slipshod about relinquishing it early on . . .

So you may want to ask someone: *Do you feel that tension when we're together?* Otherwise, on this typically solemn occasion, you may be stepping to Kierkegaard's malevolent tune of all matters handy, easy, and neat—and way too much of a good thing.

Rhodes Scholar *(Picaro)*

> *And when hee hath the kernell eate,*
> *Who doth not fling away the shell?*
> John Donne

You are always the first-rate fellow
striding the room, professing,

your craggy words passageless,
mind's bastion. You don't even know

how to drive a car. You once chopped
off your fingertip with a paper-

cutter. You let the more exotic girls
drive you home, to town and airports.

You womanized each term like a man
gone mad for miscellany. The girls

found out about each other, and wrote
you a letter signed by all three.

One of them made a cake for the man
whose professional life was above

reproach, whose birthday was the day
after St. Valentine's: a debit-red cake

iced white, decorated with two whole
confectionized measures of your bassoon

sonata. You held court at intermissions
and wowed them at concerts—

at home you lied to the ladies,
while fearless and sound in *Who's Who*.

She Finds He Is Standing Before Her

after Yeats

Those words, no token of your pause,
Sung out counter to your standing there:
Poor surrogate words, at odds
With the stuff of eye-beams,
The real affair.

A Chastisement for John Donne

> *So, if I dreame I have you, I have you,*
> *for all our joyes are but fantasticall.*
>   Elegie X, "The Dreame"
>
> *Yet, love and hate mee too....*
>   "The Prohibition"

I want to despise you,
that your wife
died upon birth
of her twelfth child.
But I can only
marvel, instead,
at your conceits.

Was it your con-
ceit that awed
her so? Was it
that which held
her down, "love-
slain," caught in a
feminine compromise?

Did it help you write
that she, with child
nearly every
year, held
her tongue and
let you love,
let it all happen?

O John.
The paradox of
this death
staggers your own
metaphysics. It's

"owner bee
of thee one hour"
murdered in
her bed. Dear Anne!

When death lifted
her last child
from arms that seemed
never to abstain
from yours, she canon-
ized herself,
and left you to
realize
that even the best
Petrarchan conceit
can only play,
and love, among words.

You See

what our words are,
after all—paroxysms
of the hottest desire; how love
transmutes; encoded murmurs.

When I say
desire it's not
that clichéd stuff.
Not anything you've
heard before. Not sex.
Not fond regard. Enough
to say that intercourse
of the sensual kind
would overstate our case.

Though I could lie
beside you for hours,
quite still, or rolling over
and over verdant knolls,
grassy and prolix,
your hardness unraveling
the paradox of which I speak.
Yes—intercourse would be
too much. Or not enough.

On the Road

> *What comes is not to be avoided*
> *What goes is not to be followed*
>   Master Daibai
>
> *That's the trouble with love. People think it involves rights.*
>   Philip Wylie, *Tomorrow!*

You will still see the sky
in common—companionate—
belt of Orion
gibbous moon
quavering stars
you can't go too far
for me to keep loving
the roomy expanse
between us. I adore a good oxymoron,
like *bittersweet* or *loathsome charm* or Shakespeare's
"*heavy lightness.*" Neither will I look for you
nor you present yourself.
Keep going. I won't see you
anytime soon. Or at all.

Long Shot

> *Today by happenstance at a Tucson gas station I saw
> a man—now a historian—from our own history of
> passing reckless billets-doux in study hall*

At the moment he looked into her face
and closed the years, he let his hand
drop that was already searching
for another cigarette, and returned her stare.
All their recent missives, the phone calls
and an ongoing speculation did not help this moment.
And he did not help her either, but stood there, waiting.
She knew she could not now expect a *deus ex machina*
bearing her self-possession. But she wanted to stay like this, looking
at him in just this way. Before she got into her car she smiled at him
in the way one would before an embrace.

Just Divine

> *You go to my head,*
> *and you linger like a haunting refrain;*
> *and I find you spinning round in my brain,*
> *like the bubbles in a glass of champagne—*
> Haven Gillespie

I don't want to leave any of that behind
—though it will take one wild divining rod
to dip the presence of these thoughts underground.
Living (or dying) without you near—willingly, but the ruminations!
Just what is it we get to keep? I plant these poems
in the primeval forest that you inhabit.
Other times we are at separate tables, separate counties.
I heard you on KQED at Moe's Books in Berkeley
with that terrific voice of yours, reading
about your 48th birthday in Jerusalem
—and abortive rescues in high water
put to music, the American experience
you never thought you'd have.
And you are the American experience I'm having
that overtops the pines and birches of Flagstaff, Arizona.

About Desire

*Preferences are harmless; we can have as many as we want. . .
[but] We have to see that everything we demand
(and even get) eventually disappoints us.*

Charlotte Joko Beck, *Nothing Special*

If we have distance
our desire
won't let us demand,
much less get.
The delight lies in missing
something. Or someone. Yeats
said (was he thinking of love?),
"Be secret and exult,
because of all things known,
that is the most difficult."
In the garden we may spy something
we missed before—a thing we *must* have.
But the core of it's this: Demand satisfaction
in practice, exercise, action, and you attach
to dismay. Satisfaction is that glorious unspeakable
thing that freely comes to me arising from distance and missing
(in Kōshō Uchiyama's words, "when I open the hand of thought").

Blindsided By Andrei Codrescu

I've never seen the man
and won't
and wouldn't
his radio voice
too potent
too strong
playful leviathan of words
publishing that leviathan
of books
sexy Romanian accent
thoroughly American man
this era's Nabokov
in operose achievement and genius
and today's essence of Beethoven
in language
context
dynamics
though even more audacious
in doing the crucial work
against expectation.

Yes—caught unprepared
as I read and listen
knowing
this writer is a prize
in my generation
and knowing furthermore
my own status
as an unashamed
sapiosexual.

With a dual emphasis in English and music, **Susan Stevens** studied voice, bassoon, and comparative literature at the University of Redlands and creative writing at Northern Arizona University. She has taught literature and creative writing on the Navajo reservation and several campuses, including Eastern Arizona College where, partnered with the Arizona Commission on the Arts, she directed the Visiting Writers Series. In federal positions covering 25 years with the U.S. Army, Navy, Marine Corps, Social Security Administration, Forest Service, and Bureau of Indian Affairs, she finished as an editor for *Engineer: Professional Bulletin for Army Engineers.*

Her poems have appeared in collections including *Seems, Northern Arizona Review, Agnes Scott College Writers Festival Magazine, George Wright Forum: A Journal of National Parks and Reserves, Voices on the Wind, Prescott National Forest Granite Tablet, The Reach of Song,* and *Reflections,* and prose in *The Story Teller: The Society of Southwestern Authors.*

www.ingramcontent.com/pod-product-compliance
Lightning Source LLC
LaVergne TN
LVHW041513070426
835507LV00012B/1528